Amy H. Johnson

THE FANGIRL FILES

True Tales and Tips from the Fandom Frontlines

© 2015 Amy H. Johnson
All rights reserved.
Printed in the United States of America

ISBN 978-0-9969719-1-1

Cover art and design by Sund Studio
Book design by Maureen Moore, Booksmyth Press

Dedicated

to my mom who taught me everything I know
and has supported every crazy Fangirl idea
I've had and often enhanced it,
and to my dad who got an autograph of a member
of A-ha for me and gifted me with binoculars
"for viewings of Larry Mullen Jr."

Thank you both for a wonderful childhood
in our house in the woods.

Contents

Introduction   11

1
You Know You're a Fangirl If . . .   15

2
Little Fangirl in the Big Woods   18

3
Anatomy of an Obsession   23

4
Wall of Men   26

5
Team Spirit   28

6
In Honor of Keanu Charles Reeves   30

7
Proper Concert Etiquette   33

8
Shower, Rattle and Roll   37

9
The Truth Is In My Freezer   49

10
A Fangirl's Guide to Meeting a Celebrity   53

11
Ultimate TV Boyfriend   58

12
In Defense of Boy Bands   61

13
U2:23   64

14
Finding Your Heart's Desire and Following It   71

15
Targeted Tips   80

Epilogue   85

Acknowledgements   87

Fan / noun / an ardent admirer or enthusiast (as of a celebrity or a pursuit)

Girl / noun / a female child, from birth to full growth

Fangirl / noun / a girl or woman who is an extremely or overly enthusiastic fan of someone or something (first known use, 1934)

—*Merriam-Webster Dictionary*

Fangirls aren't groupies looking to land a famous boyfriend. We are passionate, devoted, slightly crazy, but harmless women who adore a band, actor or TV show so much that we go to some wild extremes to celebrate the objects of our affection.

INTRODUCTION

I often tell people that I'm a born Fangirl. It is in my genes. I can't deny it any more than I can deny I have brown eyes. My grandmother used to skip school to stand in line for Frank Sinatra tickets. Years later my mother screamed for The Beatles at Shea Stadium. Nearly a decade after that I was the proud owner of my first record under the shade of a Christmas tree: Shaun Cassidy and his blonde feathered locks having captured my six-year-old heart every week on "The Hardy Boys."

Since then it has been a natural part of my personality to fall in love with TV shows, bands, actors and singers, and to put my energy and attention towards them. It never seemed unusual to me because I saw my mom, Linda, do it, and she was always supportive of each new face I brought to her attention. That acceptance made me feel secure about how much I loved my objects of affection and, in that sense, made me comfortable in my own skin. It helped me learn to trust myself because I wasn't wasting energy on hiding my affections or defending my crushes. Many times she got right into a fandom with me; sharing interests in music, taking me to concerts, and making trips to cool record stores to find Japanese fan magazines and rare 12-inch singles from Europe. My mom may not have always understood my attraction, but that never stopped her from encouraging me. My dad, Steve, played a part as well. I don't think he has ever been quite sure why my mom and I are the way we are about bands or actors, but he was the one who gave me a custom-made bag that said "Taylor" when I had a mad crush on Duran Duran bassist John Taylor and bought me a James Dean cookie jar when I discovered *Rebel Without a Cause*.

So being supported at home made it easy to be a Fangirl.

The next step was finding like-minded people who shared my attraction to the Flavor of the Month or Year or, in some cases, Decades. Once I had a partner-in-crime, the sky was the limit. Young girls have endless amounts of energy to spend on learning their crush's favorite colors and foods; they have vast imaginations for how their wedding to said crush would look and how adorable their make-believe children would be.

Now my friends and I do those sorts of things as employed, tax-paying, home-owning women! No matter what age, once you are no longer solo in your interests, there's no telling where you and like-minded individuals can go in terms of extreme fandom. And the Internet has only made things worse. In the old days, when your favorite show was off the air or your favorite band was between tours, you just made do with your old magazines until things started up again and there was new material to gush over, or you focused on another interest because there was no new product to sustain your attention.

Fandom can now be a 24/7 job. YouTube not only provides primary source material, like interviews and show clips, but also the whole wide world of fan videos. Your beloved TV couple's best romantic moments set to your favorite Indie rock song? Why yes, please! And Facebook has a page for everything. You just join in "liking" it and *voila!* Updates on everything from in-store appearances, talk show interviews and magazine spreads are delivered to you instantaneously. There are photos, blogs and fan fiction—you name it—it is out there and there's lots of it. And really, has there ever been a better invention for fans than Twitter? The fact that I can now know what John Taylor is doing at *this very minute* because he is telling me (and thousands of other followers) still boggles my mind.

In all honesty, it is a blessing that those things didn't exist in the formative years of my Fangirling because I don't know that

I could have survived it. I could barely contain my excitement when certain videos came on MTV and I sure as hell wouldn't have been able to focus on schoolwork with concert ticket pre-sales to plan for and updated blogs to read—the sheer wealth of available information now means there is never a moment to turn off your fandom.

Instead, I "came up through the trenches" and it has made me a better Fangirl. I've learned patience and loyalty (years between records and tours will do that for you). I've learned about compromise and acceptance (when your best friend claims your favorite band member before you do). I learned how to laugh at myself and take ownership of my decisions (don't ask me how much I paid for that 'N Sync ticket). And I have come to understand that no one and nothing should stand in the way of what makes you happy. If it's a song, a singer, the cute guy who plays the brother of that other cute guy on a CW show, an engrossing teen vampire series—whatever it is—pursue it, love it, be proud of it. I'm proud of being a Fangirl and I hope after reading this book you'll be proud to be one too.

1

You Know You're a Fangirl If . . .
A 25-point checklist

1. You celebrated idols' birthdays by having cake and/or preparing their favorite meal as if they were coming over to celebrate.

2. You waited outside a tour bus in below-freezing temperatures or stood against a fence in the middle of the night or been in a General Admission line before the crack of dawn not once, but many times.

3. You had your pre-teen bedroom wallpapered with a plaid pattern so your pictures of rock stars could be lined up easily along a straight line.

4. You called the hospital every single day when your teen idol was injured, and your dedication got you grounded when your mother saw the phone bill.

5. You commissioned a custom-made item as a wedding present for your favorite band member and his new bride and carried it to multiple concerts until you found the right bodyguard to deliver it for you.

6. You got a tattoo of a song lyric by your favorite band written in a band member's handwriting, which you got from a photo on the Internet.

7. You scheduled your entire college semester and summer internship around a concert tour.

8. You made a gingerbread likeness of your TV Boyfriend and tweeted him a photo of it.

9. You baked a cake to celebrate an album release with the cover of the album on the cake.

10. You threw a themed party to celebrate a TV show premiere or finale.

11. You flew cross-country and back in less than 48 hours to see one concert.

12. You sent out Christmas cards of yourself posing with cardboard cutouts of your favorite band and signed them, "love, me and (insert band name here)."

13. You ate at a dining establishment owned by a rock star, owned by the relative of a rock star, or frequented by a rock star.

14. You visited the alma mater of your idol and bought a school or team shirt.

15. You traveled alone to a foreign country for the first time to see a concert by your favorite band.

16. You purchased items of clothing similar to ones your idol owns.

17. You walked on the street your celebrity crush grew up on.

18. You recorded multiple seasons of a TV show and copied every single scene of your favorite on-screen couple for a master library of their romance.

19. You bought a bed solely because it looked like the one in a music video by your all-time favorite band.

20. You took a twelve-hour, whirlwind trip to see a concert film, even though it was arriving on DVD in the mail later the same week.

21. You bought an iPhone for the express purpose of being able to follow your celebrity crush on Twitter and listen to his podcasts.

22. You custom-ordered M&M's with song lyrics for your friends on Valentine's Day.

23. You went to a record store on the day of an album's release despite being so violently ill with the flu you had no recollection of how you got home.

24. You made a floor to ceiling photo collage on a wall in your apartment of your favorite TV couple with accompanying quotes that you cover up to protect during hurricane threats.

25. You have enough activities surrounding your love of bands, TV Boyfriends, and rock stars that you literally can write a book.

These are all things that either I have done or women I know have happily, willingly and proudly participated in. If you see one, two or nine things on this list that you have done or would totally do, then congratulations, you're a Fangirl!

2

Little Fangirl in the Big Woods
That 70's childhood

Some Fangirls are born while others are made. I am certainly born to it. I come from a legacy of Fangirls—my grandmother and mother directly and, on that same side of the family, a great-aunt who once had an entire room in her house dedicated to Judy Garland and a cousin who regularly goes to sci-fi and fantasy conventions where she decorates her hotel room door with themes like "Male Celebrities as Desserts."

I grew up in the seventies in a funky house my father had built in the middle of the woods. He was a Southern California boy who wanted a life away from the suburbs and strip malls where he could "get back to the land." My mother was a New York girl educated in Manhattan who followed him to this land and lived there bravely for the next nineteen years. We had a menagerie of dogs, cats, birds, hamsters, chickens and a cow.

In contrast to what kids grow up with today, we may as well have been living in the colonial ages in terms of technology. We had a black and white TV, a rotary phone, a record player and for a time an 8-track player. If we missed something on television, there was no way to see it again. If we missed a call, there was no way to retrieve a message. If we wanted to hear a single song repeatedly, we had to keep getting up and dropping the needle back down on the vinyl.

Yet despite the minimal media access in my house, I still found things that excited and sparked the little Fangirl in me. I was thoroughly intrigued by variety shows. I loved "The Sonny and Cher Comedy Hour" and "Donny and Marie." If there were cheesy musical numbers, glittery costumes, group dances and corny skits with celebrity guest stars, I was in front of that TV transfixed every week.

"Donny and Marie" particularly entranced me. Donny and Marie Osmond are a brother and sister singing duo who are part of a large singing family. (I really shouldn't have to tell you this, the Osmonds are practically American Royalty!) I didn't care much about Donny because I was so captivated by Marie. I didn't know it at the time, but Marie was only a teenager during the series. If I had known, I would have certainly wanted her as my babysitter. Instead she was a beautiful lady on TV who had sparkly ball gowns, satin jumpsuits and a different hairstyle every week and sometimes even within one episode. She was snarky to her older brother and, even though I didn't necessarily understand the jokes, I liked her sassy attitude, and she sang, danced, acted, roller-skated *and* ice-skated on her show.

These were all things I enjoyed doing despite having no glamorous wardrobe, camera-friendly brother or TV audience to perform for. As an impressionable six-year-old, I knew that What I Wanted to Be When I Grew Up was Marie Osmond. Not necessarily a singer/dancer/actress/professional sister, but *actually* Marie Osmond and live my life on a soundstage with backup dancers and my own ice-skating rink. At that age there is not really a mechanism in your head that says, "You can't *be* her, you can be *like* her." So the closest I came to my dream was playing with my Donny and Marie dolls in their matching purple and silver outfits despite a distressing event in my childhood known as "The Marie Doll Theft" that involved my pristine Marie doll being suspiciously "exchanged" with a friend's

Marie doll with a broken thumb on the eve of my so-called-friend moving away.

Anyway, in 2013 I got a chance to see Donny and Marie at their Las Vegas show and I cannot deny that, when Marie first graced the stage, my Inner Child had a bit of a mini-freak-out that she was ACTUALLY IN FRONT OF ME! And I am thrilled to report that once after tweeting her about the fancy boots she had posted a photo of, she replied to me. I wish I could telegraph that bit of information to little girl me as she fussed over her imposter Marie doll with the broken digit.

As much as I loved Marie, someone else eventually supplanted her. This is the era I refer to as "The Sandy Years." A family friend took me to see *Grease* in a movie theater and I was hooked. I came home and talked about nothing but Pink Ladies and "Greased Lightning." I ended up with an album and photo-book of the movie that were dog-eared from so much time spent studying the liner notes and re-reading the book. I loved good-girl Sandy played by Olivia Newton-John and Wanted to Be Her When I Grew Up. By then I was able to make a distinction between Marie Osmond as a real person and Sandy as a character in a movie, but that did nothing to curb my longing to be a blonde Australian in a 1950s high school.

I saw the movie again as a college student and was shocked at its raunchiness. My friend Heather and I agreed that our parents must have decided it was easier ignoring the songs full of sexual innuendo that we little girls were singing all the time rather than explaining why they were inappropriate. I wouldn't have cared anyway because my favorite song was Sandy's "Hopelessly Devoted to You," an innocent tune which she brokenheartedly sings at a sleepover while wearing a pale blue ribbon in her pretty hair. This satin ribbon was *it* for me, the fashion statement to end all fashion statements! Despite being a brunette, I truly believed a blue ribbon could make me look like Sandy, so I put one in my hair and sat on my toy chest looking longingly towards the floor in a re-enactment of Sandy sadly watching the car race at the end of the movie. Although I had no witnesses, I am positive I looked *exactly* as she did in that scene. Several years ago, I went to a *Grease Sing-a-Long* with my friend Janis and I wore a blue satin ribbon in my hair for old times' sake.

When I wasn't busy with Marie or Sandy, I was in love with Shaun Cassidy. He of the blonde, feathered hair and pearly white smile. Loving Shaun Cassidy was made easy by the fact that he was a Double Threat: he was a pop star and a TV star. I could listen to his music while staring at his dreamy face on the cover of his album and then tune in weekly to "The Hardy Boys" to see him solve mysteries with his TV brother played by Parker Stevenson. Again, there was no MTV or Internet. If I wanted to see Shaun Cassidy I had one chance a week to get my fix. I could listen to his album endlessly, but not go to YouTube to watch clip after clip of him crooning "Da Do Ron Ron."

Shaun certainly paved the way for the next Big Crush of my young life: Rick Springfield. Rick took Shaun's dual-career concept and turned it up a notch. He was not just a pop star with a weekly TV show but a rock star on a daily soap opera, and not just any soap, but the most popular one at the time, "General Hospital." Not only were there albums to listen to, but a show to watch after school every day! And the cherry on the top of this particular hunky-Australian-born-rock-god-also-known-as-Dr. Noah Drake sundae was that he came to fame right at the start of MTV so I could see him in music videos too. It was like having my cake and eating it multiple times a day. Rick Springfield's concert was the very first one I ever went to, thanks to my mom who shared my adoration of all things Rick-related.

While it may sound like all I did as a child was watch dorky variety shows, obsess over movie musicals and watch cute guys on television, in fact I was actually a balanced kid who had Barbie dolls, loved animals, rode my bike, played with friends, and read a lot. I particularly loved the *Little House on the Prairie* books because they were about a little girl who grew up in the woods just like I was doing. I identified with the famous Garth Williams cover illustration of young Laura lovingly cradling her doll in a cabin built by her father. I suppose if a kid today were looking at the way I lived in 1970s New England, with no technology and few entertainment options, it would be similar to how Laura's life in 1800s Wisconsin must have looked to me.

My childhood was good, filled with typical little girl activities as well as some aspirations I think were pretty sweet: to be a wholesome and talented young lady with great outfits in love with an attractive fellow who sang on television. In the realm of childhood dreams these didn't seem too outlandish and, in the big woods where I lived, they opened up a whole world to me that went beyond black and white TV and 8-track players.

3

Anatomy of an Obsession
Phase one to DEFCON

Phase One
<u>Say:</u> "Oh look at/listen to that! Kind of interesting!"

<u>Do:</u> Google the name of the entity that sparked your interest.

Phase Two
<u>Say:</u> "This is really growing on me. What else is out there about it?"

<u>Do:</u> Go online to Wikipedia/YouTube/IMDB and do research. Find essential Twitter or Instagram feeds and follow.

Phase Three
<u>Say:</u> "Wow I really love this! I have to tell my friends about it!"

<u>Do:</u> Post links about your interest on your social media and casually start dropping the topic into conversations. Get overexcited when a friend says, "Oh, I like that too!"

Phase Four
<u>Say:</u> "Oh my God! They are touring/releasing a DVD/going to be on a late night talk show!"

<u>Do:</u> Buy a concert ticket, binge-watch a series, stay up and watch the late night talk show because you absolutely can't wait to watch it on the DVR tomorrow.

Phase Five
Say: "I am in LOVE! I must have more!"

Do: Start playlists on YouTube and add to them rigorously. Right click photos and save liberally. Spend many hours on official Twitter feeds, fan blogs and Tumblr.

Phase Six
Say: "This is the BEST EVER IN THE ENTIRE HISTORY OF THE WORLD!! What is *wrong* with everybody who doesn't *get* that?!"

Do: Stop casually mentioning your interest to friends and begin talking incessantly about it all the time to everyone. Share links to videos and photos and articles and expect instantaneous and enthusiastic responses from the recipients.

Phase Seven
Say: "I need more stuff! The Internet is not enough!"

Do: Go to iTunes and buy the entire back catalog. Go to Amazon and buy DVDs and books and calendars. Start buying terrible magazines you never read, but will read now because they feature your idol in an issue.

Phase Eight
Say: "There must be others like me. This is really popular! Others must love it as much as I do. Where the hell are they?"

Do: Lurk at official sites. Join online fan clubs. Choose a username that will be identifiable by fans and post treatises on song lyrics, comment on recaps, create your own fan videos and write your own fan fiction.

Phase Nine

<u>Say</u>: "Anything that is NOT about this intense love is just a distraction that is keeping me from spending more time on it! Why am I so *tired*?"

<u>Do</u>: Notice how the multiple tabs open on your computer are somehow related to this intense love when it is 2:30AM and you have to be up for work at 6:30AM.

DEFCON

<u>Say</u>: "I love this so damn much I can hardly remember a time before I loved it and how in the world did I even exist without it making my life a happy and joyful place full of melodies, laughter and hotness?"

<u>Do</u>: Fly across the Atlantic to see a concert. Plan a trip to visit a friend who just happens to live in the same hometown as the object of your affection and use your Christmas Club money to fund it instead of buying presents. Meet strangers on the Internet in the town where your favorite show is filmed and then visit the shooting sites with them. Learn to live with sleep deprivation and a near-constant hemorrhage of cash and know it is always worth it.

4

Wall of Men
The handsomest wall of all

I transferred to a women's college my junior year. At the end of my first semester, my boyfriend of three years dumped me long-distance for a girl I was suspicious of from the very first time he ever said her name. After the breakup and the weeks of friends propping me up, I decided to rearrange my room to get rid of any bad juju he had left behind. I also decided to resurrect a youthful pastime of putting up pictures of cute, famous boys to moon over because I'd had it with real boys at that point. Thus the Wall of Men (WoM) was born.

The first incarnation was only up for the last semester of my junior year and was pretty basic—building from just above where my pillow sat to just below where the wall met the ceiling. Some of the fellows on it were so totally 90s, such as Evan Dando of The Lemonheads and Antonio Sabato Jr. of "General Hospital." There were also pretty male models, headless well-chiseled torsos from Calvin Klein underwear packaging, and funny guys I idolized, like Steve Martin and David Letterman.

My senior year, the WoM went from Fairly Impressive to Really Awesome. For one thing it was nearly triple the size of its predecessor. It was practically wallpaper with nary a space between pictures and reached from my bed to the ceiling. It was a joy to sleep under it and I often found friends and assorted hallmates standing in my room with their eyes glazed over in awe (or possibly horror).

My friends and I wasted a lot of time on that wall. A. Lot.

Of. Time. We discussed which guy was the hottest and which picture we'd take if the dorm caught on fire. If any of us had flunked out of school, we would have had that wall to partially blame. The rest of the blame would be on "Beverly Hills, 90210" repeats that aired during dinner time and seemed to require so much of our focus that doing homework before or after was hard (and frankly not as much fun)!

Several years ago, in the process of getting divorced and as part of my recovery from a bad marriage, I changed my furniture around to get rid of that bad juju again. Then I remembered the WoM and how happy it had made me, how my friends were giddy when I posted scans of it on Facebook. So I made another one in my home office, not quite as all encompassing and more flexible with corkboard squares so the pictures could be rotated out based on whomever I thought was the dreamiest at that particular point in time. It was tidier and I figured if a grown woman was going to have pictures of cute boys adorning her walls at least they better be nicely arranged and Pinterest-worthy.

5

Team Spirit
Rah rah rah! Sis boom bah!

Do you watch sports or have a favorite team? Sports fans sure love their teams. I live in New England, home of champion baseball, football, hockey and basketball teams, so I am well aware of sports fandom! Sports fans watch games on TV and listen on the radio. They go to home games and travel to away games where they holler and cheer and buy shirts and merchandise with their team logos and favorite players' numbers. They learn endless statistics and scores and follow trades and drafts and they even invent fantasy teams.

My bands are my teams. I watch them on TV and always listen when they're on the radio. I go to concerts two hours or 2,000 miles away and holler and cheer. I buy t-shirts and paraphernalia, CDs and magazines, and I read everything, learn anything I can about them. I love U2 the way some people love the Red Sox. I love Pearl Jam the way some people love the Patriots, I love The Killers the way some people love another team I can't think of because I don't follow sports. I'm into music.

For some reason, obsessing over sports is totally acceptable while obsessing over music or bands or TV shows or actors is less acceptable. The feminist women's college grad in me believes it has something to do with sports being more male-dominated and therefore "normal". I think these lines are getting a bit fuzzier with social media and celebrity news dictating more and more of the pop culture landscape, but it still stands that, when I see a stadium of people in freezing cold weather, some shirtless and painted with team colors, watching a football game and loving the players and the game with all their hearts and souls while waving signs and crying over losses, I really don't see how that's different from my friends and I waiting in a long line in cold weather to see a concert and then crying with joy afterwards at the experience we just shared.

Whatever makes you happy, whatever you are passionate about, and whatever fulfills you and brings you closer to others with the same loves is a good thing. You may memorize decades old pitching statistics while I compile playlists based on concert set lists. You may have a wedding designed around love for the Chapel Hill Tar Heels while someone else may have a Twilight themed wedding (and people have)! At least we love something and there's nothing at all weird about that. (Well, painting your naked chest in 12-degree weather to scream at a bunch of athletes for hours on end is a bit weird!).

6

In Honor of Keanu Charles Reeves
Giving charitably in the name of movie stars

Keanu Reeves. He's an actor, a pretty actor—not necessarily a pretty *good* actor—but I would argue he's had moments that often get overlooked because his looks usually outweigh his talent. But I don't love Keanu for his good or bad acting or for his handsome features, dark shiny hair and exotic name. I love him because he brought me one of the greatest gifts in the world: my friend Sarah.

In my senior year of college, I had a huge poster of the movie *Speed* in my dorm room. I'm not a fan of action movies per se, but there are action movies that I admit I enjoy: *Die Hard* (the first), *Gladiator*, *The Bourne Trilogy* and *Speed* are on that short list. Actually I was pretty impressed with Keanu in *Speed*. He turned his blank stoner persona into a believable movie cop and beefed up his physique to pass from just pretty to hot.

So one day my door was open while I was likely wasting time down the hall and when I returned to my room there was someone standing just inside the door where the poster resided. She was petting my *Speed* poster. Yes—petting it. No, it was not three-dimensional or printed on fabric or any other material that would cause someone to reach out and touch it. That poster petter was Sarah. We introduced ourselves and started talking and that conversation has pretty much never come to an end. It turns out we had a lot of things in common and over that year we became such good friends that we were roommates in Los Angeles after graduation and lived together again when we both ended up in Boston. Our similar demeanors, senses of humor, interests and ability to find each other endlessly hilarious—plus our belief that we'll probably end up sharing living quarters again in a nursing home—is why we call ourselves "Heterosexual Life Partners."

But before all that, there was Keanu and there was *Speed*. We spent many hours discussing his beefy arms and debating his style of movie rage versus our other shared crush, Brad Pitt (Keanu = explosive! Brad = slow-burning!). And the only thing that got us through our second semester History of Political Thought class was the "*Speed* Movie Quote Challenge" on the elevator ride up to class. This involved each of us coming up with a quote from the movie that we hadn't used yet on our twice-weekly ride. Did anyone in the elevator know what we were doing? No, but that didn't stop us from cracking ourselves up—a trait we share to this day. Indeed, often when we're together, we end up in hysterics which people around us find either entertaining or really damn annoying. A guy at the Apple store once told us we were the "most fun customers" he'd had all day, while another time a guy on a bus trip muttered as we got off, "There goes the party." Yeah, buddy—THERE IT GOES!

So the Year of Keanu culminated in something that I still can't believe we not only tried, but we got away with. Our college was eager to usher us graduating seniors into the wonderful world of alumnae—specifically alumnae giving. Starting in January we got nearly weekly letters encouraging us to start donating money to show how much we supported our education. That was all fine and good, but we were already giving them a lot of money to support our educations by being in school. Giving more when we barely had post-graduate jobs lined up was not high on our priority list.

But then we got an idea: we would give them money, sure. But we would give the money in honor of Keanu Reeves. If we could give it in honor of parents, teachers and professors, why not give it in honor of the man who had not only given us so much entertainment, but our very friendship? So we each wrote a small check and jointly filled out the pledge card and dared our Advancement Office to actually cash it and print his name in the program that would go to classmates, parents and esteemed alumnae. And we were thorough: we gave the address of his talent agency for the school to send him notice that a donation had been made in his honor, we used his middle name, and in the little box that asked us our relation to the honoree we wrote "Actor."

Then we waited with giggles and bated breath to see if they would contact us and tell us to get serious. In all honesty the day we got our thank you notes notifying us Keanu would be receiving an acknowledgement of our gift in his honor was nearly as exciting as the day we got our diplomas from our prestigious college. We never got a note from Keanu thanking us for thinking of him, or even asking, "Who are you and what is this?" but that was fine. We got his name printed in the program and, hopefully, all across the college constituencies that year there was a double take or two at the movie star name nestled in with the other honorees.

Our joint Keanu crush has since gone dormant although we will always hold a special spot in our hearts for him and his Sexy Serious Action Star Face glaring from the poster that brought us together. Twenty years later we still haven't given up doing silly stunts in the name of Fangirling and we continue to always be entertained by one another.

7

Proper Concert Etiquette
Minding your live music manners

I go to a lot of concerts. I've been going to concerts since I was a kid and I'm sure I'll be going to concerts for many years to come. So after all my years of concert going, I've designed a list of concert rules that, I hope to God if you're near me at a show, you abide by. Otherwise, we are going to have words, high-pitched, disapproving words.

> **Get there on time:** People do not enjoy moving in and out of the aisle and missing the opening song while you check your ticket because you absolutely could not skip the concession line.
>
> **Stop getting food:** It's overpriced and there is no reason you HAVE to eat that pretzel during "With or Without You." (It's also the #1 reason you are not getting there on time.)
>
> **Don't text your friends during the songs you don't know:** If the show isn't worth your undivided attention and well-spent dollars, then the exit signs are all helpfully lit.
>
> **Do not talk throughout the show:** People pay a lot of money to see the featured performer, not to listen to you. If you want to hang out chatting with friends, please stay home instead of treating a concert as your overpriced social hour.

Empty your bladder first: I have been known to not drink at all pre-concert so that there is absolutely no need to miss a minute of the show for a bathroom break. Between that and the dehydration from all the singing and dancing, believe me that first post-show gulp is amazing.

Stop arguing with security: Unless they are being completely unreasonable, they are doing their job and that job is not to allow you to push your way in front of everyone else because you think you are entitled to the best view in the house.

Drunk girls, step off: Because you're cute and drunk and spent hours before the show getting wasted, and then used your Cute Drunk Girl act to worm your way to the front because Dopey Boys think Cute Drunk Girls are hot, you do not want to piss off the hardcore Fangirls who have been standing all day long to get to that prime spot you are weaseling your way into.

Do not stay seated: I just do not get this. WHO SITS DOWN FOR A ROCK CONCERT? If you are not physically impaired, there is no excuse for this unless the headliner is sucking. And if you still insist on being the killjoy who must sit, please do not expect us to join you in our seats.

Knock it off with the booze: It's expensive and crappy and when you dance around drunk you spill it on the rest of us and then you need to go off to pee 30 times and, with every booze-related disruption you cause, the more your concert neighbors are fantasizing about punching you in the face.

Ladies dress for function, not fashion: Sure you look sexy in those platform heels and push-up bra. Is that comfortable to stand around in all night shaking your booty? Do you believe someone on stage will look out and notice your short skirt and go, "There she is! Where has she been my whole life?" No, they will not (unless you are Courteney Cox and you are in a Bruce Springsteen video and, it should be noted, she dressed for comfort!) You're going to be on your feet and you're going to want to be able to walk at the end of the night.

Guys, leave your wife or girlfriend alone: So you were dragged along and don't want to be there. Don't spend the show bitching about how lame the band is. Don't belittle your significant other for her crush on the lead singer. Don't hang all over her demanding her attention because you are too insecure to let her have fun ogling a rock star for two hours of her life.

Couples, no making out: Especially if you are in front of anyone and your locked heads are blocking their view. If you're so turned on by the music, save yourself the money and stay home playing the CD while you get amorous.

Watch the show and stop documenting it for your social media: If you are filming every song to put on YouTube instead of experiencing it, snapping photos to instantly post on Instagram, tweeting the set-list, checking-in on Facebook, taking selfies with your friends during the concert or WORST OF ALL filming yourself singing and dancing with the band behind you as if you are the star attraction of the show, GET OUT NOW.

Stay until the lights come up: Sure, getting out of the parking lot is a pain in the ass and we all want to get home at a reasonable hour. But don't ruin the encore for the rest of us by wiggling your way out of the aisle during the last moments of music or, even worse, wiggling out and then when the encore starts, wiggling back in to get back to your seat. Just stay put until every last note is played!

I may sound like a bitch, but more and more shows I go to lately are like parties and not cool, fun parties, but annoying ones full of drunk people talking too loudly and bumping into you with pretzels and wandering around looking for the bathroom. If you are there just for the expensive experience of getting drunk on terrible beer and being able to tell people that you saw this band (which you didn't because you were too busy talking and eating), you're ruining the experience for everyone who is there to hear the music and see a band they love and that is the very definition of "not cool."

8

Shower, Rattle and Roll
A bathroom fit for The King

It's the same old story. Girl goes to Graceland. Girl discovers a love for Elvis. Girl buys an Elvis shower curtain in Memphis to mark this newfound love. Girl makes an Elvis bathroom in her first adult apartment. We've all been there, haven't we?

OK, perhaps not all of us. But while it may not be a tale as old as time, it is a true tale that happened to me. After graduating college I drove cross-country with three friends towards a final destination of Los Angeles where we would start our post-graduate lives and work in the entertainment industry. On our way we had a few must-see-stops: Washington DC, the Grand Canyon, Las Vegas and, Graceland, former home of one Mr. Elvis Aaron Presley, The King of Rock and Roll.

We were all eager to see this hallowed land of American idolatry, but the excitement we experienced once we were there was far more than we anticipated. Let's just say we arrived for our tour as intrigued tourists and left almost eight full hours later with theories on where and how Elvis could still be alive, a full-blown, high intensity love for all things Presley, and weighed down by bellies full of chicken fried steak from the Visitors Commissary.

I will admit that my particular enthusiasm for seeing Graceland was based almost entirely on the fact that U2 had filmed a segment there for their concert-documentary film *Rattle and Hum* in the late 80s and, having watched it many, *many* times, I was ready to see the sights my favorite band had seen. The movie contained a touching scene of drummer and my über-crush Larry Mullen Jr. fretting about Elvis' grave and pondering whether it was right to be able to visit a resting place as a tourist attraction. My enduring love for All Things Larry meant I clearly had to stand at the spot he once stood as those deep thoughts furrowed his handsome brow.

The tour, narrated by Priscilla Presley on headphones, led us from room to room and I excitedly glimpsed spots from the movie and took photos because it was the first time in my life I had ever stood in the same place as U2 (even if it was years after the fact!). Priscilla's soothing voice telling us about the best of Elvis, the displays of his memorabilia defining how much he truly changed pop culture, and Elvis tunes playing softly on every part of the property all worked to brainwash us into Elvis fanatics by the time the bus took us back to the Visitors Center.

There we saw his planes, cars and a driver's license, which guaranteed he would never have forgotten his address as Memphis had renamed the street Graceland sat on Elvis Presley Boulevard. There was a small postal window where you could send mail and we bought postcards and wrote very excited messages to friends and family with an expected Graceland, Memphis TN postmark—only to later discover it was just a Memphis postmark since Graceland on Elvis Presley Boulevard sadly does not possess its own zip code.

By this point we were easy targets for the Graceland gift shop. We wanted anything and everything Elvis because he was the greatest entertainer EVER after we had just happily drank all the King's Kool-Aid, but we found that the shop only carried official merchandise approved by his estate. That meant pricey stuff that was a lot less cheesy than we had hoped for. We didn't want classy Elvis items; we wanted the crazy crap you always hear about, like imitation Elvis Vegas sunglasses or velvet paintings (although I did have to talk Sarah, a new college graduate without a permanent job, out of a $70 Elvis beer stein she wanted).

So we trudged around until we found a store that had the kind of crappy trinkets we wanted and that is where I found the Elvis shower curtain and deemed it the perfect first purchase for my new apartment with Sarah in L.A. It was young, pelvis-shaking Elvis in bright and garish pink, blue and yellow, but to make the bathroom a true Elvis Bathroom and not just a bathroom with an Elvis shower curtain there was more decorating to be done.

Up went an Elvis Presley Boulevard street sign over the sink; there was a Mississippi River Boat cup from a cruise we'd taken in Memphis; a framed publicity photo of a young surfing Elvis in his white swimming trunks hung on the wall; and at some point I acquired an Elvis beach towel that was black and therefore looked an awful lot like an actual velvet Elvis painting.

The Elvis bathroom did not make it past L.A. but that doesn't mean I stopped loving Elvis. After the grip of Graceland lessened its hold on my affections, I developed an appreciation for the man who I once heard a host on a VH1 countdown show say, "…invented women fainting for rock stars." Several years ago, Sarah and I saw the *Viva Elvis* show in Las Vegas—a Cirque du Soleil production that interpreted his life through his music and incredibly inventive acrobatic maneuvers. Once again, we were back in love with Elvis and emptied into the extremely expensive gift shop clutching our purses close to us for fear of spending money we still didn't have on Elvis memorabilia we still didn't need. We did, however, make kissy face poses on either side of the massive Elvis bust outside the theater. We also realized we each had an Inner-14-Year-Old-

Girl-who-grew-up-in-the-1950s who just adored Elvis. Mine is named Betty.

Betty should be pleased that even though I no longer have the shower curtain or the almost-velvet-Elvis towel, I do have a No Parking Except Elvis Fans sign on my basement door, right around the corner from my *Viva Las Vegas* tin wall hanging. Elvis forever!

A wee Fangirl and her first crush, Shaun Cassidy, Christmas, 1977

Glamour shots with Rick Springfield, Cape Cod, 1982

Finally meeting Marie Osmond—sort of! Las Vegas, 2011

The epic Wall of Men, 1994-1995 Edition

Hopefully, Smith College spent our Keanu Cash wisely

Elvis Bathroom,
7130 Hollywood Boulevard,
Los Angeles, 1995

With Sarah and the deliciously scented Mr. Jason Priestley, Los Angeles, 1995

Wise words from Mr. David Duchovny

The Golden Globes actually gave me a backstage pass!

Introducing the fifth Backstreet "Boy" at Fenway Park in 2011

The lifelong musical journey begins!
(and check out those 1985 ticket prices)

In 2009 with my mom celebrating a dream come true—
U2 in Dublin!

A homemade, hand-decorated, rock-star autographed keychain, Brandon Flowers of The Killers

Two very cold, very determined, very happy Fangirls finally get their Brandon Flowers photo! With Jill in New York City, 2010

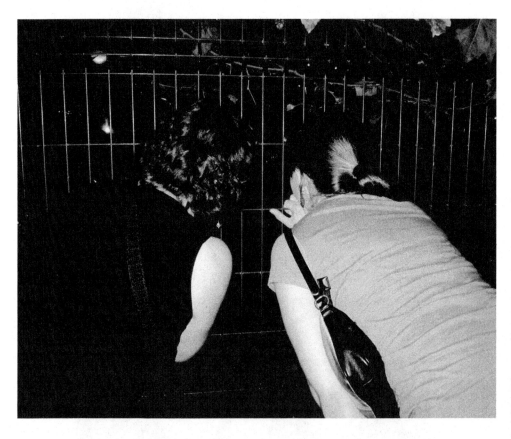

With my favorite Fangirl, my mom, Linda, peering through a fence at Boy Bands in Canada, 2011

9

The Truth Is In My Freezer
Possessing Agent Mulder's DNA

I'm going to tell you a story that I fully admit is crazy. It takes place in Los Angeles, so you know some weird stuff is going to happen. L.A. is where weird goes to flourish and become cool and end up on the cover of *US Weekly*.

The story starts two days after my friends and I arrived in L.A. having driven cross-country after graduating college. Along the way we'd experienced Dolly Parton's Dollywood theme park, re-enacted an Eagles hit on a corner in Winslow, Arizona, and stayed in Caesar's Palace in Vegas where having a phone in our bathroom was as exciting as the glittering view out our window.

On that second day, we were volunteers at a charity carnival hosted by many celebrities, which was a pretty exciting way to start a new life in Hollywood, particularly for us who were all celebrity obsessed. Our jobs were not glamorous—we led around folks dressed like cartoon characters (actors have to start somewhere and it worked for former El Pollo Loco chicken Brad Pitt!). We got lucky in that our particular characters (Tweety and Sylvester) were lazy and liked to stop and rest a lot.

This gave Sarah and me ample time to look at the celebrities who only a few weeks earlier we'd been watching in the living room of our house at our alma mater. Talk about surreal! We were particularly fixated on David Duchovny, the newly minted star of the still-cult-but-soon-to-explode-into-pop-culture show "The X-Files." However, we'd never actually watched the show believing it was too creepy and it aired on Friday nights when no college girl should be home watching television.

No, we were looking for David Duchovny because he had been in a so-bad-it's-good movie called *Kalifornia* (yes, that's with a "K") with former El Pollo Loco chicken Brad Pitt. In this so-terrible-you-can't-help-but-quote-it movie, Duchovny is a writer who wants to drive across the country with his photographer girlfriend and visit famous serial killer sites and write about them. They can't afford the trip alone so they get some strangers (Brad Pitt and Juliette Lewis) to come along with them. Their bad teeth and thick heads make them very "white trash" in comparison to the writer and his artsy girlfriend.

Conveniently Brad is an actual serial killer and, while David is musing on what makes killers kill, Brad is killing people en route. I'm sure you can guess that things don't turn out so well and there's a dénouement at one of those old Nevada test sites full of bomb blast dummies, which is both eerie and, given the fact that Duchovny would be chasing aliens on TV for the next nine years, kind of ironic. So we made our way up to David Duchovny and told him how we had just driven across the country and that our favorite movie was *Kalifornia*. It is fair to say that a look of alarm passed over his handsome angular face. We chatted and took our pictures with him and I was thrilled to see that he wrote on my photo, "Amy—Don't pick up any hitchhikers."

Fast-forward a few months and another friend from college moves out to Los Angeles and scores some jobs and one of them turns out to be Production Assistant (PA) on the "Golden Globes," the delightful award show where TV and movie stars mingle and drink copious amounts of alcohol on live television. I was intensely jealous that I didn't have the same opportunity, but at the last minute they needed more PAs so I worked all weekend at the "Golden Globes." It was fascinating seeing how it all came together and imagining re-seating Duchovny and Pitt closer to each other so some sort of "Let's make a sequel to *Kalifornia* with a K!" conversation could happen over champagne.

The celebrities who present have to rehearse, so I scanned the schedule for people I wanted to see and then made sure I had "work" to do in the ballroom when they came in. By this time I had started watching "The X-Files" and was totally obsessed with the show, so seeing Special Agent Fox Mulder again was very exciting. As he stood chatting and drinking water from a Styrofoam cup, I loitered around and made myself look busy (along with plenty of others who also had better things to do) and when he got called up to do his bit, he put down his cup and walked to the stage and that's when the aforementioned crazy happened.

Did I watch him rehearse? Oh, sure I did. But I had kept my eye on his cup from the time he put it down to the moment I wrapped my hands around it and left the ballroom. What was I doing with David Duchovny's used cup, you ask? Will I make it worse if I tell you it still had water in it and I found a baggie and bagged it as if it were evidence of my craziness and put it in my car and when I got home I stuck it in the freezer?

My cousin and fellow "X-Files" fan Laurie dubbed this "The David Duchovny Backwash" and, while she informed me I was insane, I definitely noted a bit of pride in her tone. I had no idea what I was going to do with it. Today I could sell it on eBay, but that didn't yet exist, so before I moved back East, I gave it to a L.A. friend who, believe it or not, was far crazier than I was. In fact, I would not be surprised if that girl still has it in her freezer.

My friend who got me the PA work at the "Golden Globes"

eventually got a job at "The X-Files" and she brought me to a party where I re-introduced myself to David Duchovny who, bless him, pretended to remember he'd met me months before at the charity carnival. We pitched the idea of a *Kalifornia* sequel named *Konnecticut* (where the surviving characters drive back across America) and he thought it was hilarious. (I should also mention he'd had some celebratory beverages so perhaps everything was funny to him at that point.) He did offer the following magical words, "Wanna see my Brad Pitt impression?" and then launched into a scene from the movie as Brad Pitt. So basically, our night was made!

In my own defense I'd like to point out that many years later "The Big Bang Theory" would have Leonard Nimoy Fanboy Sheldon Cooper LOSE HIS MIND when he was gifted a napkin with Nimoy DNA on it, which he could use to possibly clone his idol. So while I do admit my cup-and-backwash stealing was slightly creepy, the idea has made its way into mainstream pop culture. Clearly my craziness was just ahead of its time.

10

A Fangirl's Guide To Meeting a Celebrity
10 tips for the perfect experience

A fan is happy to go to a concert and leave after the lights come up. A Fangirl knows that the end of the show is the start of a long night outside a tour bus hoping to get a chance to see their favorite band member and maybe share a moment that can be captured by pen or picture.

Over the years I've been able to meet a quite a few celebrities. Sometimes it was luck, sometimes I paid for the opportunity (God bless the Meet & Greet), but most of the time it took a lot of dedication, perseverance and the withstanding of a variety of weather conditions to meet the object of my affection.

Here are some tips I'd like to share for achieving a perfect experience with your idol.

1. **Be prepared**. Before you leave your house, pack up something you want signed—a photo, a CD cover or, if you really want to impress, bring something unique like that rare vinyl import from Japan with only 500 copies in existence.

   Emergency option: Use your ticket stub.

2. **Supply your own writing implement.** I recommend Sharpies because they are easy to fish out of your bag and they leave a nice, thick autograph.

   Bonus tip: Your pen has now been held in the hand of your crush and you can go home and frame it.

3. **Ask for a photograph and have your shot ready to go.** Don't hold up the guitarist by getting your camera app open when all he really wants is a shower and has nicely stopped to say hi to you and your friends after entertaining you for the past two hours.

   Bonus tip: If a minder or bodyguard type says, "No pictures," ask the performer anyway. It takes a little longer than a handshake, but they may not even know that you were told not to ask and, unless they have their own policy against it, they'll probably do it.

4. **Make contact.** Look them in the eye and hold out your hand to introduce yourself. Don't be rude just because you're star-struck.

   Success Story: When I met the stars of "The Vampire Diaries," I made sure to do this and it bought us more time and earned my pal Julie a special greeting and her own handshake from star Ian Somerhalder!

5. **Don't demand contact.** Follow Step 4, but don't ask for a hug! Listening to them, watching them, and planning imaginary weddings with them doesn't mean you actually know them. Stick with the handshake and don't make things uncomfortable by demanding more intimate forms of contact when they are being gracious enough.

   Exception: If the celebrity is instigating the hugging, then by all means wrap your arms around that boy and hug the hell out of him!

6. **Smell them.** Yes, it sounds creepy, but I can't tell you how many times I've met a Cute Famous Boy and later been asked by multiple women, "What did he smell like?" and

then been heckled if I couldn't name a particular fragrance or conjure up a romantic image. ("Why, he smelled like the beach at sunset!") Sniff when they are giving their autograph or listening to a girl tell them how much their first album got her through the breakup with her college boyfriend.

<u>Success Story:</u> Jason Priestley, he of Brandon Walsh "Beverly Hills, 90210" fame, inadvertently taught me this trick when I took a picture with him and he smelled good enough to have his own cologne called "Smells Like Jason Priestley."

7. **Don't hog them.** Yes, you love and adore them and waited hours and hours to have this moment, but, once you've had it, you need to step back and let other fans get their moment as well. They all have bags stuffed with cameras, CD covers and Sharpies too!

<u>Cautionary Tale:</u> I once saw Joey McIntyre of New Kids on the Block give a drunk girl a finger wagging and send her off after she belligerently pushed her way into a line to meet him a second time. You want them to remember you—just not remember that they don't want to see you again.

8. **Stay calm.** Of course you're excited—it's really exciting meeting someone famous whom you admire and adore. However, you don't want to miss the moment because you are freaking out so much it all goes by in a blur. Nor do you want to scare the hell out of him by screeching, "OHMIGOD!! OHMIGOD!!" in his face.

<u>Tip:</u> Breathe and tell yourself, "I can freak out later." Then remind yourself to focus on the moment.

9. **Be memorable.** You don't have a lot of time so stand out from the others who are repeating the same old, "Oh my God I love you! The show was so awesome!" Say something that will capture their attention. I recommend being sassy and not sucking up.

   Success Story: I wasn't up for being a sycophant after freezing in the dark one New York City night for three hours to meet Brandon Flowers of The Killers who was greeting fans on his tour bus. So when I noticed the large number of bananas he had on the bus I blurted out, "Got enough bananas?" Then as my friend Jill and I posed with him for a picture, she remembered she wanted a memento from her bag included in the photo and exclaimed, "Oh shit!" so the combo of teasing and swearing put us miles apart from regular fan behavior!

10. **Show them what you've got.** No, I don't mean flashing and being an aggressive pervert. That's not cool. I mean, if you made a gift, give it to them or show them a memento from something they inspired you to do, like visiting a place of importance in their life. Let them know that you're not just a fan you are a Fangirl!

    Success Story: When I met the Backstreet Boys, I brought a photo of myself at a camp where member Brian Littrell had spent time as a child. I visited once when I was in his home state for their concert and it took him a minute to recognize the place, but then he got excited when he realized where it was. I experienced a special moment of reminding him of something he'd forgotten and he felt the warm nostalgia of being reminded. Win-win!

So there you go—put in the time, be prepared and stay calm. Try to envision how you'd behave if you were meeting a stranger for the first time who wasn't famous. You likely wouldn't start crying and demanding hugs and shoving others out of the way to get to them. That would be weird and rude, right? Celebrities are people too, so just approach them as calmly and politely as you would any other human being (even if you're screaming your head off internally). When you meet the man of your rock star, TV or movie dreams, be respectful and enjoy the moment. Then freak out and start plotting for the next Fangirl adventure!

11

Ultimate TV Boyfriend
One stands above them all

I have a boyfriend who is so dreamy—tall, dark hair and blue eyes, not classically handsome, but good-looking in a way that is appealing. Of course looks aren't everything—he's also clever, charming, funny and a real romantic who will protect a girl's honor and remember all sorts of little things about her. He's just the best and he never disappoints me because he's not real. Perhaps if you were a fan of what I call Cheesy Teen Dramas in the mid to late 90s, you know who I'm talking about: The Best Friend, The Romantic Underdog. That's right, ladies, it's Pacey Witter, the sexy scoundrel of "Dawson's Creek."

If you are a female who watched The WB Network between 1998-2003 or if you know an adult woman who will admit to watching Cheesy Teen Dramas, then just say "Pacey" and watch her reaction. I guarantee there will be some sort of swooning involved. The character was the not-at-all-perfect best friend of the perfect lead who was Dawson, of course. Pacey was the comedic foil always ready with a witty barb who propped up the romantic lead. He wasn't meant to get the girl or be the hero. He was the sidekick, plain and simple.

However, they cast brash young Canadian Joshua Jackson as Pacey and he was far more captivating than milquetoasty James van der Beek who played Dawson. Ugh. DAWSON! He was self-absorbed, entitled and, worst of all, he was boring. Dawson had few struggles and no demons and it made him less interesting than just about every other character on the show.

Pacey meanwhile had so much charisma and great chemistry with everyone and he had capital I Issues: he was a poor student with a difficult home life and a troublesome temper combined with a white-knight complex. Those traits made him interesting and a character to invest in.

In the third season, Pacey falling in love with his nemesis, tomboy Joey Potter, catapulted Pacey from cute, funny, sidekick into "OMG I wish he was my boyfriend!" territory. Joey was supposedly fated to be Dawson's girl, so this storyline was pretty daring in that it challenged the show's own premise, but nothing is better for a Cheesy Teen Drama than romantic angst, particularly of the love triangle variety. What made Pacey's corner of the triangle so appealing is that he suffered. He knew he couldn't be with the girl he loved because she "belonged" to his best friend and he felt disloyal for having those feelings in the first place. He really tapped into that adolescent longing for someone. It was not only appealingly romantic because Pacey was dreamy as all get-out, but because it plucked at the heartstrings of any Inner Teen Girl who ever had those seemingly hopeless fantasies about a crush.

I got sucked into this plot to a ridiculous degree and I let my Inner Teen Girl take over and go nuts as only an Inner Teen Girl in the body of a grown woman can do. I joined message boards to talk about the show and searched out spoilers so I could discuss what was coming with other fans; I made online friends and spent hours, *oh my God so many hours,* chatting with them about this one fictional boy! When the show tried to put their genie back in the bottle by dismantling the well-written romantic arc they'd set up for Pacey and Joey, I did something that I never thought I would do: I started writing fan fiction about it. And if *that* weren't crazy enough, I actually went public with it and, if *that* weren't already ridiculous, I actually gained a small degree of what could be considered fame (or maybe it was infamy!) from the specific fandom that cared about such things.

So I have outed myself as a writer of "Dawson's Creek" fan fiction. It was great fun and cathartic and I really sharpened my writing skills doing it. The inconsistent writing on the show made me a better writer and Pacey Witter as a protagonist gave me so much to work with. I can't help but be proud of what I did in spite of the fact I was a woman nearing my thirties who feverishly wrote alternative versions of a show about teenagers that was aimed below my demographic. I also made some great friends and the friendships have far outlasted the lifespan of the show. My mom always says, "Never underestimate the cute boy factor," which means that women will pay attention, develop interests and follow all sorts of paths they may not have imagined when there's a cute boy leading the way.

While the show has been over for years and my days of writing about it long past, I still love Pacey. He is my Ultimate TV Boyfriend. My belief is that he will forever remain The Ultimate because, with the show over, there's no way he can do anything to ever disappoint me or make me stop adoring him. And in a world where women now get million dollar book deals for their fan fiction about a popular fictional character, perhaps I was just, once again, ahead of my time.

12

In Defense of Boy Bands
Never breaking your heart or making you cry

I love Boy Bands.

Yeah, I said it! If there are four or five cute guys singing snappy love songs and dancing in unison in flashy outfits, I am all over it.

And don't give me the usual backtalk because I have heard it all:

- *They're manufactured!* So are the singers on "American Idol" who seem to get a pass despite their success on a reality show.
- *They don't write their own songs!* Neither did Elvis, The King of Rock and Roll.
- *They can't sing!* That's just nonsense.
- *They are hardly Boys or Kids anymore!* Why doesn't anyone ever say this about elder statesmen the Beastie Boys?
- *Only teenyboppers like that kind of music!* That is false. I don't know many teens, but I know a lot of grown women with jobs, families, mortgages and retirement portfolios who love Boy Bands.

I didn't always love Boy Bands and back in the 80s when the New Kids on the Block appeared on the scene I had zero interest. My teen preferences were cute English boys who sang moody music. American boys singing bubblegum pop and selling lunch boxes need not apply. Then I reached my late twenties and the world was filled with Boy Bands and I couldn't resist even though I tried. I scoffed and listened to my "real music" but secretly I indulged in the Backstreet Boys' "As Long as You Love Me" whenever it came on the radio on my walk to work.

My roommate and I both got swept up in this pop culture moment. At a certain point, if you had walked into our tiny apartment, you would have been forgiven for thinking it was a den for pre-teen girls. Unlike teenage girls though, we had disposable income and no curfews. This meant we could buy seemingly unlimited magazines, books, posters, calendars, trading cards, dolls, and every other piece of marketing paraphernalia you could think of and even an entirely new piece of shelving just to house our Boy Band collections.

We also went to a lot of concerts and drove long distances. We spent an exorbitant amount of money on 'N Sync tickets. We went to Kentucky to see the Backstreet Boys and roamed the former high schools, childhood homes and places of employment of two native members. Once we spent hours going to different area colleges and buying school shirts on which we ironed numbers and Backstreet members' names as if they were a team and hand-delivered them to their hotel when they toured Boston. We may have been far out of the target audience for these bands, but we didn't care. We loved the music, the dancing, and all the guys. We discovered there was an entire sub-culture of adult women who felt the same way and kept it secret out of embarrassment thinking we were "too old" for the bands and the music.

That was over a decade ago, but I really haven't changed in my love for Boy Bands. I went to see Super-Mega-Boy-Band NKOTBSB (New Kids on the Block + Backstreet Boys) multiple times in 2011, once even going as far as Canada. I was gleeful when I was one of 50 people invited by New Kid Joey McIntyre to attend his private Christmas album release party in a swank Boston hotel that same year. At historic Fenway Park where NKOTBSB performed, I splurged on a Meet and Greet, finally meeting the Backstreet Boys then joyfully danced in the pouring rain during the New Kids set (who clearly, I had changed my mind about!)

Some women love Boy Bands and are loyal to them for their entire lives—through school, boyfriends, college, children, marriages, divorces and jobs. My theory is that's because Boy Bands say all the things females want the real males in their lives to say, but never do. Those sentiments and promises of love, fidelity and devotion appeal to girls of all ages—from the young ones who've never had their hearts broken to the older ones whose hearts have been bruised. Boy Bands get a bad rap because they sing pop music and dance in unison. But it's called pop music because pop is short for popular and it's popular because it's catchy, fun, light, frothy and usually you can dance to it. It makes people happy and it has nice melodies and lovely harmonies. So what if it's not "serious" or "important"? There is plenty of room in the world—and in my own music collection—for bands that "matter" and make music with social impact or serious sentiments. Sometimes though you just want to dance or emote in your car with dramatic hand gestures (which is one of my favorite pastimes because no one can actually see me, right?). This particular type of music got me through a lot of tough times and it makes putting up with Real Boys a lot easier when you know a Boy Band will be there to catch you when a Real Boy lets you down.

And don't tell me you don't know the words to "I Want it That Way" because I won't believe you.

13

U2:23
A lifelong musical journey

I am not religious. I don't go to church and there isn't much that I can say I believe in on a spiritual level. My father is an excommunicated Mormon and my mother a lapsed Catholic. Because of my parents' distance from organized religion, I never experienced much in the way of church or God and I don't feel that I missed out. I got to sleep in on Sunday mornings when friends had to go to services and I didn't have to worry about confirmations or confessions or knowing my prayers or even having "church clothes."

That is not to say I have not experienced spirituality, just that my experiences have come from a very different place and, to those who practice traditionally, that place may seem strange or even sacrilegious. To me, it is a perfect fit. So where do I find what I do not find in church and God? I find it at the Boston Garden, or the Worcester Centrum. Once I found it in a muddy racetrack in Saratoga, a few times at Foxboro Stadium and one glorious night it was at a soccer stadium in Ireland. From arenas and stadiums and venues new and old I have found love, salvation, joy, hope, peace and community when I see U2 in concert.

I first heard of U2 when I was 11 and my mom had recorded a concert of theirs from the radio when they were a baby band and she asked if I had heard of them. I hadn't so she pressed play and that was it. I was in. My love for them has lasted nearly my entire life and their music has been a soundtrack to every era in my history: *The Unforgettable Fire* album got me through a rocky college relationship; "Breathe" was my anthem during my separation and eventual divorce; "Where the Streets Have No Name" never fails to lift me up and hold me there always with tears! U2 has been my most dependable comfort and steady constant for over 30 years.

Since that introduction, my mom and I have shared our U2 fandom and have seen them together in concert 23 times between 1984 and 2015 (a number which to hardcore U2 fans isn't much, but to casual fans is impressive). Every single concert has been an emotional and exciting ride that we've shared together. The entire show is not in itself always a religious experience—but there is always a moment—one chord, one verse, one second where it changes from a concert to something more. The crowd and the band become one entity and the music delivers us all to someplace higher than where we are standing.

Here are just a few of my favorite moments from those shows. There are really no words to accurately capture what these experiences mean to me and what it's meant to share in this musical journey with my mom, other than to say they have been some of the greatest gifts of my life.

JOSHUA TREE 1987, WORCESTER MA: I am with a friend up in the balcony while our mothers score near-front-row seats. We're young girls surrounded by a lot of inebriated adults. One guy behind us hollers for "Gloria" all night long and, when they finally play it in the finale, he's ecstatic as we all are. But soon after it's over the same guy either forgets or doesn't care because he wants another go and starts screaming, "Play Gloria!!"

ZooTV 1992, Boston MA: It is St. Patrick's Day and we're seeing U2 at the Boston Garden. Can you get more Irish than that? Our seats are terrible, so we sit on the floor, our feet hanging over the entrance below us. College-age boys with backwards baseball caps sit alongside us singing "One" as if their lives depended on it. On the way out of the show, the audience continues a long U2 tradition of singing their song "40" and all our voices echo off the ancient Garden walls.

ZooTV 1992, Saratoga NY: We stand all day long to get into a racetrack-turned-venue so we can stand all night long in mud up to our ankles. It all becomes worth it when the band comes down to the small stage in the field in front of us for "Desire." In those moments we are the closest we've ever been to them and actually see the color of their eyes and it feels like the thousands of other people melt away and we're at an intimate gig with a few other folks.

Elevation 2001, Boston MA: From the floor I look around and see the entire arena. I can't make out faces, but I can see movement and, during "Where the Streets Have No Name" I notice everyone is moving, *everyone*. We are all moving as one entity and it looks like the building itself is alive and breathing and screaming and dancing. It is so phenomenal to see that it is hard to look back at the stage. I am ecstatic to be part of something so alive.

Elevation 2001, Boston MA: We are at the fourth show out of four at the former Boston Garden, now named after a corporation. We almost didn't make this one together. I had a ticket and my mom didn't, so I was faced with the impossible choice of going without her to see U2 for the first time ever, or not going at all. Then my best friend Rachel appeared with a ticket she couldn't use. The drama and joy of the last few days welled up as they closed with "Walk On". All arms were raised as Bono called, "Alle alle, alleluia" at the end and tears ran down my face.

360 2009, DUBLIN IRELAND: We've done it! We've made a twenty-four-year-old dream come true and here we stand with 80,000 others from around the world and around the corner on a cool Irish summer night. The roar of so many people welcoming the band home as they descend onto the stage intensifies with the rumbling drums of "Breathe" that launch the show. It had been a hard year with my marriage ending, but this song and its words have inspired me and I am so grateful they are what welcomed me to one of the greatest nights at the start of my new life.

360 2009, DUBLIN IRELAND: Thousands of people descend on Dublin to see the hometown boys. The band knows this and easily weed out the locals from the tourists by launching into "The Auld Triangle" and suddenly a massive stadium full of people from around the world becomes a dark little pub with those boys from the north side of River Liffey leading a round of a classic Celtic tune.

360 2009, DUBLIN IRELAND: The day is full of violent rains that end before the show and leave a rainbow and an evening sky of crimson and pink. No performance of "Where the Streets Have No Name" will ever match this one. As the traditional red lights bathe us all, I hug my mom because we've been

on this ride together for over two decades and now we've done what we once thought impossible. We've seen U2 in Dublin!

360 2009, DUBLIN IRELAND: It is the song we hope for every single tour, every set list. We mourn when it's not played; we are ecstatic anytime we are lucky enough to hear it. It is beauty and sadness, hope and love in one elegy. We aren't people who pray, but every day leading up to the Dublin show we pray that we'll hear it on their home soil, in their hometown, among the people who lived and breathed the song and the heartbreak that it inscribes, that we will hear "Bad." And when we do, it is the sound of our prayers.

360 2009, FOXBORO MA: We wait eagerly for what has become a highlight of this tour, the club-like remix of "I'll Go Crazy if I Don't Go Crazy Tonight." It is the most unusual, energetic, sexy thing U2 has ever done and it feels like the space-themed set called "The Claw" will rise up and take off. Suddenly a U2 show turns into a galactic disco and, as Larry Mullen Jr. comes down with his djembe (bongo) free from his drum kit and struts like the rock star he is, my mother—never a Larry fan (that being my area of expertise)—starts screaming, "HERE HE COMES! HERE HE COMES!"

360 2011, MEADOWLANDS NJ: It is nearly two years to the day that we saw U2 in Dublin at our first 360 show. Now it is a sticky Jersey summer night and pushing through the humidity to move to the music feels like work. The set list is flawless. At the very end the band pulls out a classic. Before my mind has even put together the connection, my ears and my heart know that it is "Out of Control" and my body explodes into a full-

bodied emotional, physical and mental seizure of absolute joy and delirium.

iNNOCENCE & eXPERIENCE 2015, BOSTON MA: Rachel generously gifted us with VIP tickets so we are seated an incredible five rows from the main iNNOCENCE stage. As Bono enters the arena from the back onto the smaller eXPERIENCE stage the band launches into "The Miracle (Of Joey Ramone)" and my body is overcome with a sensation that I only get at U2 concerts: my legs go weak, my heart races, my voice lets out a noise I don't recognize anywhere else—it is always a near out-of-body moment because I can never believe that we are really there, that this is really happening, that it is really them! I am overcome with joy, excitement, love and gratitude for these four men.

iNNOCENCE & eXPERIENCE 2015, BOSTON MA: The finale ends with an inspiring arena sing-along of "One" but the band lingers on stage making gestures to each other as the crowd continues to roar. When Bono comes back to the mike I realize The Edge and Adam Clayton have switched sides of the stage and traded instruments which can only mean one thing: "They are going to play '40'!!!" I yell to my mom. Sure enough they begin to play the thirty-two-year-old song that was a finale staple decades ago and the cheers grow even louder at this unexpected and moving surprise.

While organized religion is not something I feel a connection to, I do feel a connection to music. And my mother, to whom I am forever grateful for the gift of U2, has often said that U2 concerts are "what church *should* be": full of grace, love, belief, celebration and being part of something bigger than yourself. I realize these experiences are the closest to holiness I will likely ever get.

My mom also says, "There are no bad U2 shows—only varying degrees of great U2 shows," and to that I say, "Amen!"

14

Finding Your Heart's Desire and Following It
How Amy got her groove back

OBSESSION AT FIRST SIGHT

You see the face of a tall, dark, impossibly handsome stranger across a crowded room and your heart skips and breath catches as people move and laugh around you oblivious to the magic you have just experienced. In a moment you know for sure it is love at first sight. It's the same with obsession at first sight. It was September 4, 2009 and the man who caught my eye was a singer from Las Vegas fronting a band called The Killers. His legitimate non-stage name was Brandon Flowers and I had been aware of him for a few years, having been a fan of The Killers' first album *Hot Fuss,* a very-eighties-sounding throwback to the much loved moody, synthy English pop music of my adolescence. In fact, my first interest in Brandon Flowers was based on the assumption that he was British. Being the Anglophile I am and lover of moody, synthy English pop music sung by pretty boys in suits and eyeliner, I briefly got into The Killers until I found out they were from Nevada and my interest cooled considerably.

Earlier that year I had been listening a lot to their third album *Day and Age* and, at a Fourth of July party, I played the CD. One of the hostesses was also a fan so we looked to see if the band was touring. They were and we bought tickets to the fateful show that was two months to the day away. When September arrived I went to the show thinking nothing more of it than a fun night with friends listening to good music. They came out while the house lights were still on and launched into their biggest hit "Mr. Brightside." The audience was caught off guard by still being illuminated and hearing what you'd expect to be a finale. I was less confused and more thunderstruck. The back-up musicians walked on and the other three band members took their places. Then Brandon Flowers strolled onto the stage in black combat boots, tight black jeans and a black jacket with feathered epaulets on his broad shoulders. I wish someone had taken my picture at that moment because I'm pretty sure my jaw dropped wide open and not just because the man was wearing, and I repeat, *feathered epaulets*.

That was it—that was the moment—the obsession at first sight and he hadn't even sung his first note! He was intense and focused and his voice was incredible. He commanded the stage like he was born to walk it and every set of eyes in the arena watched his every move. He knew it, but somehow didn't come off as arrogant about the power he had or the fact that his voice was so unique or that he was ridiculously handsome. Yes, I noticed all this from way back in the arena because he was that powerful under those lights and on stage directing the audience from atop monitors, holding notes as if his life depended on it, stalking past his band mates to make sure that every fan was as involved with the music as he was. It was breathtaking and, when it was over, I knew something had changed. I walked in there a fan and I walked out an obsessed person.

The next morning, I woke up and grabbed my phone to go to YouTube to see him again, hear him again, relive that moment that had so gripped me the night before. Later that day when my mom asked me how the show was all I could say was, "Oh my God!" His great bone structure and carefully mussed hair along with his combat boots and eclectic style seemed to have sprung fully formed from my Inner 14-Year-Old's imagination of The Perfect Imaginary Rock Star Boyfriend. But the music is what first attracted me and my love for the band only grew once the obsession launched. For the next two years, it took me on adventures I never could have envisioned on that hot July night when I pressed the purchase button and got a ticket to the ride of my life.

FEEDING THE BEAST

If you've ever fallen in love, you know that crazy feeling: happy, silly, sort of drunk on life and completely mesmerized by everything this new wonderful person says and does. You talk about them all the time, you want to spend every minute with them and nothing they do is wrong. It's quite simply wonderful and usually makes everyone else around you think you have lost your mind.

When you fall into an obsession with someone famous, those same euphoric sensations are there, but they are entirely one-sided. The object of your affection doesn't know you exist and has no connection to you beyond the one they make with you as an audience member and fan. So instead of spending all your time with this amazing new person, you spend all your time filling every corner of your life with their image, personality and any single thing you can find or create that relates to them.

Here are just a few of the things that my obsession with Brandon Flowers led me to do in those months following the concert: make Killers Christmas ornaments filled with feathers a la the epaulets and glitter in honor of their Vegas roots; bake cookies in the shape of their K logo; commission my cousin to create laser-cut K logo key chains for my friends that I decorated with tiny gems to mimic their K keyboard covered in lights; order M&M's with their song lyrics printed on them for Valentine's Day; craft snow globes and votive candleholders with the covers of their holiday singles; purchase a purple animal print shirt, tall rubber rain boots, and black skinny jeans because they resembled items I saw Brandon wearing; decorate a gingerbread Brandon Flowers—make that two gingerbread Brandon Flowers; go to Las Vegas on a Tuesday to see his show on Wednesday, and then fly home to Massachusetts on Thursday to go back to work on Friday; travel to Las Vegas and tour any place Brandon mentioned as somewhere he liked to eat, hang out or visit and, one year, I did this *three times;* start eating nectarines because he said it was his favorite fruit.

Now lest you think I am a completely insane person, please be aware that I was not alone. Oh, no. I was with Sarah who had been at the same fateful concert and was at her own level of fanaticism for the band and with my new friend Jill whom I had met at a U2 conference a month after the Brandon obsession was born. On top of being a sister U2 fanatic, she was a fellow Killers fan and she had her own intense level of obsessing, which more often than not involved themed baked goods (she's a cake decorator extraordinaire) and narrating videos we made of our Fangirl craft projects and escapades. Online and eventually on the road, I also met more new friends who were all in the same crazed boat as I was.

On the surface it sounds a little wacky, but trust me on this: when you are at the level of adoration that I was, there is no "too much." Anything that fills your world with your object of obsession is a good thing, be it putting their pictures on your fridge, eating their favorite foods or making playlists based on songs they told an interviewer they loved. All of it makes you feel connected to them beyond just being an admirer of their work. So I didn't know the man personally and I never would, but he did occupy my life much like a relationship would. My passion for The Killers and Brandon in particular brought me into a phase of my life that I will always be grateful for because it made me creative, ambitious, and spontaneous in ways I had never been before. What followed after that September 2009 concert was several years of full-on Fangirling that filled my life with much more than I ever could have anticipated. I had no idea that custom ornaments and nectarines were only the start.

FREEZING FOR FLOWERS

I spent a lot of time standing in lines in 2010. I stood in line in Las Vegas on a casino floor next to Elvis slots, in New York City on a steamy summer day, in London with a lot of well-behaved English people, in Birmingham, England on a chilly fall night, in Boston in early winter temperatures, in Atlantic City surrounded by drunk people, in Philadelphia as a veteran of waiting in cold weather, back in New York City where I was reminded how much I don't like cold weather, and in a final line in Vegas, almost four months to the day it all began, exhausted but triumphant.

All those lines led to doors that opened up to a small venue in which Brandon Flowers would appear on his own to promote his first solo album *Flamingo*. The news of the album came out only minutes before I boarded a plane to Vegas in April 2010 to vacation with Jill and meet Kathryn and Felicity, two new friends from England we had connected with online because of our shared Killers fandom. It was almost as if Brandon himself heard my wish that he would exist in a never-ending cycle of singing, performing and being available for our dissection of his every move. The timing of the album announcement as I flew to his hometown melded with the previous months of fanaticism and instantly I knew with my whole being that when he toured I would have to see as many shows as I possibly could. I wasn't making tons of money and I had a job to go to and an apartment to pay for, but what I absolutely understood was that those things would have to co-exist with my need to see his shows, wherever they were.

Between August and December that year I saw him in concert nine times up and down the eastern seaboard, across the country and in England. I made so many travel arrangements that I could have become a travel agent. I collected frequent flyer miles and joined valet parking clubs. I wore out the wheels on a quality suitcase and came home with piles of receipts and hotel brochures that I didn't have time to deal with before I took off again. I was 38 years old and single with just enough disposable income to have the time of my life. I traveled with friends and made new ones at each stop and had the most incredible, ridiculous, exhausting, freezing cold times of my life. The shows were spectacular and full of so much energy and exhilaration that all the lines and flights and train rides and broken suitcases were well worth it.

Standing in lines didn't end after we'd gotten into the shows. There was standing around tour buses afterwards hoping for a glimpse, an autograph or maybe even a quick picture. We Fangirls (and there were many guys too whom I nicknamed "The BranBoys") stood for hours in frigid weather talking about how ridiculous it was that we were standing for hours in frigid weather, but never even thinking of leaving. All that "Freezing for Flowers" paid off and I did eventually get to meet Brandon a few times when he was generous enough to invite fans into his tour bus for a few minutes late at night to sign autographs. When this happened the first time in Boston, it was so sudden that my friends and I found ourselves slightly stunned to be facing the man himself, freshly-showered with a

Sharpie in hand. It was almost surreal to find the person I had been worshipping and chasing all over the place right in front of me, quietly thanking me for my compliments and politely answering a torrent of questions from a trio of giddy ladies.

This happened twice more. In Philadelphia, I told him I'd been to England to see him and asked him for autographs for my English girlfriends. Afterwards we learned that despite a "no photos" edict, people were asking for photos with him and he was obliging. On a bitter cold New York City night in December when Jill and I got inside the bus for the last time, we were too tired and far too cold to be gushy and went ahead and asked for and got our hard-earned, much-prized picture. I kept my wits about me during those encounters only to lose my mind afterwards. My mom and many of my friends awoke to my screaming voicemails and incoherent texts each time it happened.

Here's what I realize now that there's some distance from 2010: it was about Brandon, of course, but my crush on him combined with my Fangirl spirit created a force that quite literally propelled me on no matter how tired or low on cash or overscheduled I was. It was also about freedom after several long and unhappy years. Only one year earlier I was waiting for my divorce to be finalized. I had been married for three years, separated for one and together for a total of eight years. My ex-husband walked out one night in 2008 and didn't come back. My marriage had been tough and the ending to it was a relief, but that didn't mean there was anything easy about it because it was the end of a relationship and it felt like a failure, but it also signaled the welcome demise of a version of myself who was old before her time. I had worried about money constantly and struggled with the feeling that so many things were out of reach, like seeing Ireland or having a house or writing a book. I had felt that my commitment to my troubled husband meant I would always be taking care of him and trying to fill the holes in his psyche that could never be filled. My life would be about just keeping our heads above water and not much else.

It took me awhile to get rid of all that unhappiness and sense of futility. When I was married, there was no obsessing over bands or having crushes on TV Boyfriends because I was too busy living my challenging life, but seeing The Killers that first time was like getting hit with lightning and remembering that—damn—it felt good to love music and worship a band. It was exciting to have a harmless celebrity crush and go wild for someone famous. That autumn night in Boston led me to create a blog that helped me rediscover myself as a writer, got me to reach out to strangers who shared my interests, and make connections literally around the world. It birthed an interest in being creative in so many areas of my life and I re-established the independence I had lost. Not only was it liberating and cathartic, it was so much fun. I did crazy things that defied logic even to me, but felt necessary. During this whirlwind, my best friend Rachel would remark, "I don't know where you get the energy," and I'd always reply, "Neither do I!" I just did it all because I loved it.

Looking back I can't fathom doing some of what I did because of the planning, money and flexibility it takes, but I'm so glad that I didn't let any of that hold me back because it was one of the most fun periods of my entire life and, in a way, I was reborn. My Inner Fangirl, who at six was dreaming of being Marie Osmond, who flourished during my adolescence with plans to marry John Taylor, who had a grown-woman crush on Pacey Witter and an un-cool love for the Backstreet Boys, had been pushed down under the weight of a marriage that didn't work, but had come back out to play and to stay.

These days I have a real relationship with a wonderful guy who first saw me across a crowded room and he's kind, loving and respectful of my Fangirl tendencies. I think of Brandon Flowers now like you do an ex-boyfriend that you are still fond of and are grateful for what they meant in your life. It wasn't until long after that adventure was over that I realized I should have thanked Brandon for more than just the music or the autographs. Brandon Flowers changed my life and that's not hyperbole. Maybe all that I became after I first saw him in concert in 2009 would have happened eventually in other ways and over time, but he kick-started something inside me and made me understand that being a Fangirl isn't just something I do, it's something I am.

15

Targeted Tips
For the aspiring Fangirl

So now you may be embarking on some Fangirling adventures of your own! To ensure you have all the fun and excitement you deserve, here are some ideas and advice to help get you started:

YOU'VE JUST HAD YOUR PICTURE TAKEN WITH YOUR IDOL:

1. Look at the photo and believe in the reality of "that just happened!"

2. Immediately have a friend or a fellow Fangirl snap a photo of the picture on your screen so she has it on her phone. Now it is in two places for "insurance" should you accidently delete the original in your enthusiasm to look at it a dozen times in a row.

3. Now you can begin whatever editing, filter applying and social media sharing you are dying to do.

4. As soon as possible, go to a place with a photo kiosk and make a print (or several) so there's also a hard copy in existence.

5. Prepare yourself for the fact that once the photo is public (and not just on your private social media accounts) it may show up all over the Internet—without you in it because other fans have cropped you out to focus on your idol.

Targeted Tips 81

YOU ARE WAITING IN COLD WEATHER TO MEET YOUR FAVORITE ROCK STAR AFTER A CONCERT:

1. Before the show, go to a sporting goods store and buy some hand and toe warmers, inexpensive little packets that warm up when exposed to air.

2. After the show ends, but before you go outside, open those up and put them inside your shoes and gloves.

3. Wear sensible shoes with socks and have a hat, gloves, scarf and a good coat on. (It's a pain having all this stuff inside a hot venue, but you'll be glad you did when you're standing by a tour bus in 20-degree weather at 2AM!).

4. Huddle with your friends, take turns rubbing each other's arms or hugging for warmth.

5. As soon as your "moment" has happened and it's time to go, find the nearest all-night coffee shop and order whatever it takes to warm your body back to normal temperatures.

YOU ARE MAKING A GINGERBREAD MAN OF YOUR CELEBRITY CRUSH:

1. If you don't want to bake from scratch or don't have a gingerbread cookie cutter on hand, look for a pre-made kit at grocery or craft stores. (Note: these are usually only sold around the holidays and come with a ready-to-decorate gingerbread man and also might include icing and decorations.)

2. Select an image of your crush that you want your gingerbread version to emulate so it will be easily identifiable by other fans.

3. Line a rimmed cookie sheet with wax or parchment paper and place the gingerbread man on it. This way, when you decorate, any sprinkles or candies that fall off won't go all over the counter or onto the floor. You can then also write a message, quote or lyrics on the lining with the icing. (To do this get a small Ziploc bag, fill with icing, squeeze it into a corner of the bag, clip the corner with scissors and grip the bag above the icing to do piping.)

4. Use icing to adhere the decorations to the gingerbread. Good candy for decorating includes Twizzlers, M&M's and gummy candies. You can also add colors by mixing icing with food coloring (to make black leather pants for example.)

5. Take a picture of the completed gingerbread celebrity crush likeness and post it on Twitter or Instagram. If the object of your affection has an online presence, then tweet it to them or hash tag it with their name to get their attention.

YOU ARE PREPARING TO SEE YOUR FAVORITE BAND IN CONCERT:

1. Confirm you have your ticket or whatever forms of required identification to get your ticket at Will Call (photo ID, confirmation #, email print-out).

2. Use a small cross body bag that you can wear during the show. Make sure it has compartments to keep things separate should you have to fish for them during the show in the dark and zippers so it all stays in there!

3. Pack any toiletries you may find yourself in need of—eye drops, lip gloss/chapstick, tissues, and earplugs but don't weigh yourself down with a lot of make-up.

Targeted Tips 83

4. Take some hard candies to suck on when you are dying of thirst and don't want to leave the show to get a beverage.

5. Keep a cold drink, snacks, a pack of wet wipes (to mop your sweaty brow) and maybe even a pillow and some reading material in the car in case you're stuck waiting to get out of the parking area.

YOU ARE THROWING A VIEWING PARTY FOR A TV SHOW PREMIERE, FINALE OR TELEVISION EVENT:

1. Plan a menu based around themes or names from the show. (For a Neil Patrick Harris hosted award show, for example, serve "Dr. Horrible's Hors d'oeuvres," "Barney's LegenD-airy Brownie Sundaes," or "Nachos a la NPH" in homage to his web and television series and to the man himself.)

2. If the show has a food or beverage item that is featured or is a running bit on the show, make sure to serve it or make it into a "bar." (For example: Leslie Knope and waffles on "Parks and Recreation" = Waffle Bar with different sweet toppings; Lorelai Gilmore and coffee on "Gilmore Girls" = Coffee Bar with different flavors of coffees, creams, and sweeteners in fun mugs.)

3. Plan some games around the program that everyone can play as they watch, such as a bingo for how many times a character says a trademark line or how often another character wears a recurring piece of clothing or a drinking game along the same lines, but if you want to keep it driver-safe, substitute pieces of candy for booze.

4. Ask partygoers to write down their predictions for the program before it starts and read them afterwards to see who

was correct. Give fun, inexpensive prizes to the winner(s) that relate to the show. (For an Oscar party have flashy "red carpet" themed prizes like candy pop rings and clip-on toy "diamond" earrings.)

5. If the show is a costume drama, period piece, or sci-fi/fantasy show, make the event a costume party where guests dress from that era or as a specific character.

Now go forth and Fangirl!

EPILOGUE

I once saw a photo of teenage girls "queuing in the rain" to get Beatles tickets in England in 1963. They are sitting on the sidewalk in front of the venue looking chilly and clutching Beatles memorabilia and handmade signs. They also have picnic baskets presumably full of treats for their long wait (which is so English and also pretty damn clever!).

I love this image of dedication and I recognize my friends and myself reflected in these girls: tired, excited, prepared and, most of all, devoted. I truly believe every woman has an Inner Teen Girl who has adoration and enthusiasm for whatever she loves. Some of us are just better at letting her out and why not indulge her? Wonderful things can happen when you let yourself go crazy for something you are passionate about and I hope this book has been a testament to that.

A lifetime devoted to TV Boyfriends, Boy Bands and rock stars has taught me that the culture you create around the celebrity object of your affection isn't just about the entity itself—it is about you: finding connections with ideas you haven't encountered before, opening yourself to undiscovered interests, and building relationships with people who share your passion. Inside your fandom you learn not just who you are, but what you like, how you work and what brings joy and richness to your life.

If you call yourself a Fangirl or just aspire to be one, then raise a glass to our foremothers in this photo, cold and waiting, undeterred in their determination to see the Fab Four. Fangirls celebrating the sights, sounds and talents of the ones they love. What a wonderful legacy to be part of!

ACKNOWLEDGEMENTS

The adage says, "write what you know" and I know a whole lot about Fangirling. But I didn't have these adventures and obsessions in a vacuum. So get ready for a long list of thanks to people who have made my writing—but more importantly, my life—better:

Tara of Create Your Life and the Dream Acceleration Program where the idea for this book first came to light.

Mandy for your never-flagging optimism that I would finish this book!

Janis for all the fun celebrity filled conversations and movie dates over the years.

Trish you are always there for panicked phone calls, common sense advice and TV Boyfriend gushing.

Andrea for 10:13 and 11:21.

The wonderful and amazing Lamont Ladies—Robyne for all the "stalking", Megan for hours of "General Hospital" discussions, Lisa for starting me on my L.A. escapades, Steph for the Boston shenanigans and Laura for the Boy Band Adventures.

Heather for always knowing exactly what celebrity story I'm talking about and never thinking anything I'm doing is ridiculous because you're often doing it about someone else.

Sarah you make me laugh harder than anyone I've ever met and there is no one I'd rather have as my Heterosexual Life Partner!

Rachel you have known me nearly all my life and have never once questioned any crazy Fangirlie thing I did but instead cheered me on. Thank you for being the best, kindest and most generous friend anyone could ever ask for.

My Lil Sis Jill you entered my world and it was as if you had been there forever. Our Crazy East Coast Girls Adventures brought a joy to my life I could never have imagined.

Felicity and Kathryn for reading, supporting and being just as insane as I was each step of the way. It was only right we all met in Fabulous Las Vegas and reunited in London.

Thank you Lauren for taking me to Vegas on a Wednesday in December so I could finish the *Flamingo* journey right where I started it.

Thanks to every friend I made in 2010 standing in lines for Brandon Flowers: Jackie, Cherish (RIP sweet girl), Katelyn, Samantha, Lisa, Kathryn W, Cat, Laura, Kimberly, Martha, Nancy, Joanne—and the various "BranBoys"—you made standing in lines far more fun than it should be!

The Friday Night Writes group—Julie, Janet, Kathy, Ted and Barry you are the most supportive and enthusiastic cheerleaders any writer could ask for. You make me a better writer and this book would not have been completed without your careful listening and smart feedback.

Julie Kushner (read her at TV Recappers Anonymous!) you can truly be credited as my advisor/consultant on this book. Thank you for all the patient support, reading, research and invaluable advice.

Acknowledgements

Adam you walked into my "office" (aka "Teen Girl's Room") soon after we met and instead of running in horror—exclaimed, "This is awesome!" Your love for me and respect for my fandoms mean the world. Thank you for being the Fred to my Ginger.

My dad Steve for building the funky house in the woods that will always be home in my heart.

My mom Linda you have always supported my crushes and fancies and said, "Do it!" when I announce a possibly crazy Fangirl idea. Thank you for continually giving me the confidence to express what I love and never feel ashamed about it.

Appreciation and love to my family, cousins and friends.

Enormous thanks to Marian Kelner for her dedicated editing, Maureen Moore for her layout expertise, Sund Studio for the amazing cover art, and Ambient Film Production and Susan Lombardi-Verticelli for my fabulous book trailer.

And to every single Object of Obsession featured in this book—my sincerest gratitude for all the talents you've given the world and the joy and inspiration you've brought to my life (and please don't take out any restraining orders!).

COLOPHON

This text of this book was composed using Adobe Garamond Pro, a graceful serif face created by Robert Slimbach for Adobe in 1989. He based it on typefaces first created by the famed French printer Claude Garamond in the sixteenth century. The headings and titles use Darwin, a display typeface created by Chilean type designer Mendoza Vergara.

The hand lettering of the title for the cover and title page were created by Kevin Alves.

CPSIA information can be obtained
at www.ICGtesting.com
Printed in the USA
LVOW04s0104070916
503449LV00032B/1355/P